RODY

Memories of Homer Rodeheaver

BERT H. WILHOIT

 BJU PRESS Greenville, SC 29614

Library of Congress Cataloging-in-Publication Data

Wilhoit, Bert H. (Bert Harvey), 1916-
Rody : memories of Homer Rodeheaver / Bert H. Wilhoit.
p. cm.
ISBN 1-57924-387-8
1. Rodeheaver, Homer A. (Homer Alvan), 1880-1955. 2. Musicians—United States—Biography. 3. Music publishers—United States—Biography. 4. Evangelists—United States—Biography. I. Title

ML429.R63 W55 2000
269'.2'092—dc21
[B]
00-036772

Photos from the archives of Bob Jones University.

NOTE: The fact that materials produced by other publishers may be referred to in this volume does not constitute an endorsement by Bob Jones University Press of the content or theological position of materials produced by such publishers. The position of Bob Jones University Press, and of the University itself, is well known. Any references and ancillary materials are listed as an aid to the reader and in an attempt to maintain the accepted academic standards of the publishing industry.

Rody: Memories of Homer Rodeheaver
by Bert H. Wilhoit

Edited by April Howze
Designed by Jamie Leong
Composition by Agnieszka Augustyniak and Beata Augustyniak

Greenville, South Carolina 29614

Printed in the United States of America

ISBN 1-57924-387-8

15 14 13 12 11 10 9 8 7 6 5 4 3 2 1

This book is dedicated to
my darling wife, Mildred Mary Wilhoit,
and my sons, Mel and David Wilhoit

Table of Contents

Preface

During the past several years, a number of Bob Jones University students have inquired at the University's archives concerning the reason for the name of Rodeheaver Auditorium on the campus. We can assume that a number of the following reasons account for the decision to name the auditorium after Homer Rodeheaver.

Homer Rodeheaver, a former associate of Billy Sunday, became a close friend of Dr. Bob Jones Sr. and Dr. Bob Jones Jr. These men were associated at the summer events of the Winona Lake (Indiana) Christian Assembly. Also, Rodeheaver had been associated with both Joneses in various evangelistic campaigns. During the early twentieth century, over twelve hundred evangelists would congregate at the Winona Lake assembly ground. Since Rodeheaver was associated with Billy Sunday for twenty years, a common interest in evangelism brought the Joneses, Billy Sunday, and Rodeheaver together. In 1942 Rodeheaver received the honorary degree of Doctor of Sacred Music from Bob Jones College.

During 1945 Rodeheaver visited Bob Jones College in Cleveland, Tennessee, and observed the crowded conditions in the chapel services. With more than a thousand students enrolled, students attended chapel in both Margaret Mack Auditorium and the regular college chapel. Rodeheaver, recognizing the vital need for expansion, volunteered to grant twenty-five thousand dollars toward the construction of a new auditorium. Since space for construction was inadequate in Cleveland, this effort was planned for Greenville, South Carolina.

The move to Greenville took place during 1947 when Bob Jones College became Bob Jones University. The new auditorium, constructed with some of the qualities of a megaphone, seated approximately three thousand. Since Rodeheaver was a member of the University's Board of Trustees, Bob Jones University donated land for the Rodeheaver Boys' Ranch in Palatka, Florida. The University President also stated that Rodeheaver indicated his plans to create a foundation to help worthy students majoring in music. Therefore, our friend Homer Rodeheaver was rightly honored by having Rodeheaver Auditorium named after him.

Bert H. Wilhoit

Acknowledgments

I am grateful to Dr. Dwight Gustafson for his evaluation and criticism, and I was encouraged by his comments concerning the usefulness of the narrative for future students. Dr. Stewart Custer also gave helpful advice and expressed interest in Rodeheaver's relaxed personality as a song leader. Special appreciation is due Emery and Jay Bopp for contributions to the cover. Dr. Grace Hargis gave kind and thoughtful assistance in copyediting this biography of Homer Rodeheaver.

Mr. Bruce Howe, a former manager of the Rodeheaver Hall-Mack Publishing Company, graciously presented photographs and vital information toward this endeavor. The Reverend Lee C. Fisher, a former manager of Rodeheaver's boys' ranch in Florida, gave helpful material toward this narrative. He and I have had a common interest in the life of Homer Rodeheaver. Dr. Bob Jones Jr., speaking of Rody as a close friend, gave some interesting characteristics of Rodeheaver, particularly his charisma and his ability to hold an audience's attention.

Mr. Allen Disbro, a member of the Winona Lake Historical Society, graciously gave his consent for the reproduction of photographs from the 1990 Winona Lake souvenir calendar. A most thoughtful Winona Lake neighbor, Mrs. Warren Campbell, presented some photographs and other helpful information that she received from the Rainbow Point sale.

I am particularly indebted to Edmund C. Gruss, writer of a valuable text on cults and the occult, and to Lyle W. Dorsett, who wrote the biography of Billy Sunday and commented frequently on Homer Rodeheaver and his activity in the Sunday campaigns. I also am grateful to Mr. Joseph Allen, director of Mack Library at Bob Jones University, for his interest in the writing of this biography and for the opportunity to do a certain amount of the research while performing my duties at the library.

Since I was associated with Homer Rodeheaver during the 1940s, I have taken the occasion to express my personal feelings and observations of this notable gentleman. I feel strongly that his personality and love of the gospel song need to be expressed for the sake of young people in this present generation.

I am grateful for the use of *Music in Evangelism* by Phil Kerr (Singspiration Inc., Zondervan Publishing House). A publisher suggested that it would be relevant to the biography of Rodeheaver to relate some of the stories of composers affiliated with the Rodeheaver Publishing Company.

Finally, I wish to express my gratitude to Mr. Roland Felts for his contribution concerning his final days with Homer Rodeheaver. Mr. Felts not only traveled with Rodeheaver during his final years as his accompanist, but he was also music editor of the Rodeheaver Hall-Mack Publishing Company before its sale to Word Incorporated.

Introduction

Who was Rody? This name was a nickname of Homer Rodeheaver, who during the early twentieth century, traveled as a song leader with the outstanding evangelist Billy Sunday.

While attending Ohio Wesleyan University, Rody was interested in music. It was there that Dr. William Biederwolf, director of the Winona Lake Bible Conference, was captivated by Rody's musical abilities as well as his "cheerleading" qualities. He apparently thought Rody would make a good song leader. Eventually Rodeheaver was introduced to Evangelist Billy Sunday, a former baseball star. In time, Rodeheaver and Sunday united as an evangelistic team.

As I sat either in the congregation or at the keyboard as his accompanist, I realized that few song leaders or masters of ceremony possessed his platform charisma. With trombone in hand, he could lead a crowd of several thousand people, drawing song from the throats of men who thought it was not "macho" to sing. He was preparing the hearts of the crowd for the message that would follow. During a school assembly, Rody would excite the students with choruses and some amusing event before the message. Although many students had never heard a Christian message before, they soon had any antagonism broken down. By the time the sermon began, the student body was ready to respond to a message from the Bible.

Rody was unique in several ways. When he moved to Winona Lake, Indiana, he purchased an old farmhouse beside the lake. He converted the house into the appearance of a ship, including a railing around the flat roof. Occasionally, we guests were entertained on the flat roof, where it appeared that we were docked at some harbor. I was told that at one time he had a sliding-board extending from an upstairs room into the lake. Thus, Rody could take his early morning dip.

I best knew Rodeheaver from his unique style of platform behavior during the annual Rodeheaver School of Sacred Music. The first two-week session I attended was in 1935. Although I enjoyed music, as an eighteen-year-old I thought some things strange. During the vocal period, the entire chorus would have vocal exercises. Such contortions as wiggling of the jaw and wrinkling of the nose were hilarious to me. I soon found out that their purpose was to help the vocalist to sing in a more relaxed way.

Ten years later I was serving as pastor's assistant and organist at a church in Ft. Wayne, Indiana. During this time our church would conduct an annual school of sacred music. We invited Homer Rodeheaver, Merrill Dunlop, B. D. Ackley, and others to perform and give instruction. It was during this time that I became more personally acquainted with Rodeheaver. Eventually I was invited to serve as his organist and pianist during the Rodeheaver School of Sacred Music. It was my joy and privilege to serve in this capacity from 1946 to 1948.

Later I was requested to serve as organist for Rodeheaver and his sister Ruth Rodeheaver Thomas in the production of Rainbow Recordings. The name *Rainbow* was derived from the chorus of one of the most famous songs of the Billy Sunday campaigns: "Every cloud will wear a rainbow if your heart keeps right." Of course, the publishing company's logo was a rainbow, and I was also interested to notice that in the Rodeheaver home the carpet and dishes bore the image of a rainbow. One of my greatest delights was accompanying Mr. Rodeheaver in the Billy Sunday Tabernacle as he conducted the Hallelujah Chorus from Handel's *Messiah.* I will always cherish those moments.

Dr. Bert H. Wilhoit

chapter one

Rodeheaver's Family and Youth

Rodeheaver's Family and Youth

In contrast to Rodeheaver's financial fortune and publicity during his latter years, he had humble beginnings. He was born in Simco Hollow, Hocking County, Ohio, and was reared in Tewcomb, Tennessee. Homer had two brothers, Yumbert and Joseph. Yumbert became a music teacher; in fact, the opera star Grace Moore received her first voice lessons from him.[1] Rodeheaver's mother died when he was only eight, and eventually his father remarried. In Jellico, Tennessee, his half-sister Ruth and his half-brother Jack were born. Homer was obliged to work early in life. He hauled logs and also drove a spike team in the coal mines. However, hard work did not keep him from getting an education. He graduated from the public school system and went on to college. He would work for six months and then attend classes the rest of the year.[2]

From boyhood, Rodeheaver's love for music was evident. Growing up, he heard young black boys entertain his mother by singing some of their spirituals. Thus Rody was greatly influenced by spirituals, which became an important part of his life. Occasionally he would sing some of the mountain ballads at picnics, but he preferred spirituals. Rodeheaver commented

> The hillbilly songs are mostly all melody . . . and lack harmony, while the Negro spiritual has rhythm, melody and harmony. The spiritual stands in definite contrast to the [mountain] ballad in that while the ballad tells a story of varied import, the spiritual has a definite religious purpose.[3]

The ability to harmonize well, without the knowledge of harmony construction, reveals the natural ability of the people who composed the spirituals. Frequently the spiritual was adapted from the sermon being preached: "It's not my brother or my sister, but it's me, O Lord, standin' in the need of prayer." Rodeheaver remarked about the spirituals, "The rhythm came from Africa with the slaves. Mixed with the culture, refinement, and religious influence of the southern white people, the spiritual was born."[4]

Besides Rody's singing, he learned to play the cornet, the bass drum, and the trombone. He purchased his trombone for seven dollars from a friend in dire need of cash. This was the instrument he carried with him to the Spanish-American War, playing with the Fourth Tennessee Band in Cuba. During World War I he used it in France while he was engaged there in YMCA work. He also used this trombone in various revival meetings, on the radio, in the Orient, and in the Billy Sunday campaigns.[5]

Left: *Homer Rodeheaver*
Bottom: *The Rodeheaver brothers, J. N. (Dr. Joe), Yumbert, and Homer, along with their sister Ruth*

Top: *Rody and his famous trombone*
Right: *Rody and sister Ruth Rodeheaver Thomas at a camp meeting*

Rodeheaver's Interest in Music Evangelism

Although Rodeheaver was unaware of it at the time, in his youth his musical interests were being shaped for his later ministry of music in evangelism. At college he was chosen as yell-leader, similar in some ways to today's cheerleader. His success as yell-leader attracted the attention of R. A. Walton, an evangelist who needed a song leader for a two-week campaign.[1] Two years later Rody's charisma attracted the attention of Dr. W. E. Biederwolf. Rodeheaver and Biederwolf were associated in evangelism for five years.

Rodeheaver's World Tour with Dr. Biederwolf

During the years of 1923-24, Rodeheaver made a world tour of Europe and the Orient. In his diaries he particularly described the contrasts of Japan and Korea. Although Japan seemed to thrive more industrially, he felt that the Japanese lacked the musical ability that the Koreans possessed.[2] The Japanese sang with somewhat of a "nasal twang," whereas the Koreans' tone quality consisted of a more "open vowel" sound. He was greatly impressed with the Koreans' potential musical ability.[3]

The Koreans made many inquiries about Billy Sunday's campaigns, his prayer life, his offerings, and so on. Knowing how Billy detested any interruptions, Rody mused about how Sunday would respond to the many crying infants during a preaching service.[4]

Rodeheaver believed that most of the Christians in Korea were doctrinally sound. He noted that the major objection of Japanese Christians concerning missionaries was the liberal indoctrination presented by some U.S. seminaries in Japan. Rodeheaver felt that this was most unfortunate. He suggested that the believers get in touch with other missionaries and boards that were doing the kind of Fundamentalist work and teaching they wanted done.[5]

Rodeheaver in the Congo

Rodeheaver also became a close friend of Arthur J. Moore, a bishop of the Methodist Episcopal Church South. The two traveled in Africa throughout the Congo. Bishop Moore wrote of this trip:

> Rody was indeed a Missionary of Music to our brothers in black. From very early in the morning until night we traveled from village to village singing and preaching the "wonderful words of life." With his spirit of helpfulness, his fine interpretation of the Christian hymns, his much traveled and famous trombone and [his] sunny disposition, he made a real contribution to the Church of Christ in the Congo.[6]

Rodeheaver was interested to find the source of the spiritual. He was convinced that its origin was not to be found in Wales, Scotland, or Africa, as some theorized, but in the southern United States. "There the rhythm was enjoined to a melody founded of Christian experience, harmonized by God's gift."[7]

chapter three

The History of Winona Lake

All the lakes of northern Indiana, including Winona Lake, are natural bodies of water. Koskiusko County, which includes Winona Lake, contains several hundred lakes. During Civil War days, much of this area was swampland. Indiana historical archives relate that the island in the lake, a portion of what later became a park, was used for training purposes by an Indianapolis regiment of the Union army. On this island was Rainbow Point, Homer Rodeheaver's residence. Originally the dwelling was a farmhouse, which Rodeheaver bought in 1912. Later on, Rodeheaver's sister Ruth Thomas and her husband Jim resided in this same dwelling.[1]

Westminster Hotel, bought by Rodeheaver and the Thomases in 1941, has a fascinating historical background. During World War I, the building was used as a veteran's hospital, and later it housed a

United Brethren publishing company. During Rodeheaver's ownership, it served both as a hotel and as the home office of the Rodeheaver Publishing Company.[2] In the late 1960s it was sold to the Free Methodist denomination, and it continued as a hotel named The Freedom House.

While the Westminster Hotel was owned by the Rodeheaver clan, I served there during the summer months as a desk clerk. During this time I became personally acquainted with a number of gospel hymn composers: Virgil and Blanche Brock, Merrill Dunlop, B. D. Ackley, A. H. Ackley, Gloria Roe, George Bennard, Griffith Jones, and Carl Blackmore.

During the early twentieth century, Winona Lake became quite famous for its summer Chautauqua activities. The Chautauqua, named for a lake in western New York, was a widespread means of disseminating culture in late nineteenth and early twentieth century America. A Chautauqua was a lecture and entertainment series including concerts and plays, often presented outdoors, in a tent, or in a structure built for the purpose.

During the Chautauqua activities at Winona Lake, many people came in horse-drawn buggies and Model T Fords. They came to hear the singing of German opera star Madam Schumann Hank and American opera stars Lawrence Tibbett and Grace Moore. One week was set aside for opera stars, another week for political rallies, and a couple of weeks for a Bible conference. During the Bible conference time, the Rodeheaver School of

Music conducted its sessions, all sponsored by charging a fee for admission to the grounds.

Before the Chautauqua seasons began, Winona Lake was known as Eagle Lake. In 1894 Dr. Solomon Dickey, a Presbyterian, was interested in having a "religious Chautauqua." He decided on Eagle Lake and purchased it with the financial assistance of his denomination. An organization known as the Winona Assembly and Summer School Association was formed. Led by a board of directors consisting of John Studebaker, Thomas Kane, and William Jennings Bryan, the association built many new structures. In time the seasonal visitors increased from thirty-five to several thousand.

Dr. Gilbert Stenholm, a Bob Jones University faculty member, related that when he was a nine-year-old boy living in Chicago, his parents took him to the Winona Lake Bible Conference. At that time several hundred evangelists were present. That number dwindled greatly in later years, perhaps partly due to the influence of radio and television.[3]

Around the turn of the twentieth century, Billy Sunday, a young baseball player who became an evangelist after getting saved, began to call Winona Lake home. It was in Winona Lake that song leader Homer Rodeheaver, pianist and composer B. D. Ackley, and forceful preacher Billy Sunday made their impact. In 1910 the Sundays built their home, Mt. Hood, in the town of Winona Lake. During April of 1914 a great fire swept the town, and in the next year came financial ruin, partly because of greatly decreased railroad revenue. Reorganization followed, and the Winona Assembly and Bible Conference decided to host several conferences. In 1920 Dr. G. Campbell Morgan founded the Winona Lake School of Theology. During the same year construction began on the Billy Sunday Tabernacle, which could seat seventy-five hundred.[4]

The latter years of the twentieth century brought renewed interest in Winona's past. Grace College purchased Westminster Hotel as a dormitory for their college men. The Winona Lake Historical Society exists to preserve the past and promote the future of Winona Lake.

chapter four

Twenty Years with Billy Sunday

It was during Mr. Sunday's appearance in Winfield, Kansas, that he first heard of Homer Rodeheaver. Sunday was greatly impressed with Rodeheaver's magnetism in coaxing a Chautauqua congregation to sing. Such community singing he had never before heard. Billy Sunday determined that Rody was his man!

Within a year Rodeheaver united with Sunday as his song leader, campaigning for souls. The personalities of the two men were very different—Sunday was blusterous and Rody was more suave. However, each seemed to compensate for the other. During their association of twenty years, they held evangelistic campaigns in many large cities of the United States. It is estimated that Rody directed seventy million people in gospel song.[1]

During World War I Rodeheaver spent a brief period in France with his trombone, feeling the call to serve his country. As a representative of the Young Men's Christian Association (YMCA), Rodeheaver, with his "talking trombone" and cheerful personality, made quite an impact on the boys in the trenches. After the armistice, Rody again united with Billy Sunday, and scores streamed to their services.

As Rodeheaver's popularity grew, he was sought after for his time and talent.[2] His many appearances on national radio broadcasts and his assistance in large assemblies for evangelical work attested to his increasing popularity. He was invited to direct the singing at the Canadian National Exhibit. He became associated with the National Broadcasting Company. Indeed, his name became a household word among those who knew him as the director of music in the Billy Sunday evangelistic team.

The Sunday team's singing and preaching were unusual compared with the practice in many of the denominational churches. The team's motive was to appeal to the unchurched. Musically, Rody was unique, particularly in presenting the simplest gospel song in a highly artistic style. He took advantage of the dynamics. During an evangelistic service, it was common for his choir to present the gospel song "Master, the Tempest Is Raging" and the "Hallelujah Chorus" from the *Messiah* oratorio. He did so in order to appeal to both the common laboring man and the person with an artistic ear.[3]

Rodeheaver had his critics, as does anyone who makes a mark on the world. He was frequently criticized by pastors for using the gospel songs "Brighten the Corner Where You Are" and "Every Cloud Will Wear a Rainbow If Your Heart Keeps Right." Rody's response was that such a song was never intended for a devotional service. Its purpose was to span the gap between the secular or popular song and the well-known hymns of his day. Its light and melodic manner reinforced the lyrics. The Billy Sunday campaigns took place in days when many blue-collar workers were unemployed. Rodeheaver felt that songs such as "Brighten the Corner Where You Are" were suggestive of an attitude and practice that men and women needed.[4]

Rodeheaver's platform decorum and appeal were uncommon. During a song service, he would frequently interject a personal incident expressing some moral thought. He delighted in telling the following story to illustrate the meaning of *co-operation.*

> Some years ago Billy Sunday was conducting an evangelistic service in Duluth, Minnesota. A Jew was run over in the iron mines. They took him to a Catholic hospital, where an Episcopal doctor cut off his leg. A Presbyterian woman there, feeling sorry for the man, wrote to Dr. Barton, who was then running a Congregational paper in Chicago, and

> asked him to put an advertisement in his paper asking someone to donate a wooden leg to this Jew in the Catholic hospital, whose leg had been cut off by the Episcopal doctor.
>
> A Methodist woman in River Forest, Illinois, saw the advertisement in the Congregational paper. Her husband, who had been a Baptist and was dead, had had a wooden leg. She telephoned for the Salvation Army captain to come by and wrap up her Baptist husband's wooden leg. He took it down to the express office, where a Lutheran express messenger delivered it to an Evangelical nurse in the Duluth office. She took it over to the Catholic hospital, and when they strapped it on this Jew, they said he had become a United Brethren. This is an application of *cooperation*.[5]

A story should be told only when it specifically illustrates something in the previous thought. Rody declared that the right kind of story will aid one in some embarrassing situations. Certainly there are moments when the audience should relax and laugh. For example, if one is introduced by flattering comments, it would be awkward not to acknowledge them in some way. Rodeheaver sometimes used this poem:

> It is my joy in life to find
> At every turning of the road,

The strong arms of a comrade kind
To help me onward with my load.
And since I have no gold to give,
And love alone can make amends—
My daily prayer is, While I live,
God, make me worthy of my friends.[6]

Occasionally during a Billy Sunday campaign, Rody would remark in his low drawl, "You know this is a Methodist trombone, and occasionally it 'backslides.' " He would also sometimes exclaim as he pulled the slide in and out of his trombone, "Just imagine! I'm being *paid* just to do this!"

Sometimes a song service inspired Sunday. Enjoying the words or the embellishment of the harmony, he would call out, "Hold it, Rody!" This would remind the listeners that Sunday appreciated a message in song as well as the preached Word of God.

Between 1909 and 1935 Billy Sunday was a familiar name throughout the United States. Certainly there were critics of his flamboyant display and conservative doctrine. On the other hand, several thousand people loyally came to his defense.[7]

Nell and Billy Sunday had hoped that their evangelistic campaigns could be arranged so that she could spend more time with their children. The gradual increase in his popularity and the increasing crowds at his meetings were more than Sunday had expected. During the years 1908-20 the contributions demanded more attention, and

Sunday realized he could not cope with all the details. Consequently, Nell Sunday came to his rescue, taking it upon herself to become the chief manager. She organized a staff of several assistants, among whom Rodeheaver and Ackley were primary.[8]

Virginia Asher, one of the staff members, did much to enhance the evangelistic effort. She was formerly a Roman Catholic, but her life was completely changed after she sat under the ministry of R. A. Torrey and Dwight L. Moody. In time she became a Bible teacher at Moody Bible Institute. Both she and her husband were effective teachers. However, Mrs. Sunday was particularly impressed with Virginia's graceful platform appearance. Her strong contralto voice made her an excellent soloist, and she also became known for her duets with Rodeheaver. The two were noted for their singing of "In the Garden" and "The Old Rugged Cross."

During a period when Mrs. Sunday was ill, Mrs. Asher was requested to take her place in various ministries. In 1912 both Mr. and Mrs. Asher worked with the Sunday campaign on a full-time basis.[9] Running these large campaigns also demanded advance work with the clergy. Nell Sunday had the enormous task of going to cities in advance to find a proper location for a tabernacle and to arrange for proper construction. She planned the financial aspect and cared for all needed expenses. Billy Sunday took no part in the advance work of the revival meetings, but he was conscious that it was a most important task.

Sunday also had no part in the selection of music during the campaigns. Occasionally in the midst of a song, he would make a comment or two. When someone sang from sheet music, he would exclaim that it "gave him chills!" He feared that such a rendition would dampen the fervency of an evangelistic service. Sunday was very spontaneous, usually letting the action create its own situation instead of deliberately building the situation. However, he would accept Rodeheaver's judgment in allowing certain renditions from oratorios to be sung.

One Welsh tenor, Evan Williams, was requested to sing before a message. The message planned had a tender appeal, but Williams unknowingly chose a song less appropriate, "Yield Not to Temptation." Rather than this song, Rodeheaver requested that he sing "Thy Rebuke Hath Broken His Heart." Undoubtedly the song made an impact and prepared the congregation for the message to follow. The effect of singing such a song along with certain gospel songs showed that the public appreciated great artistry in the presentation of simple music.[10]

The influence and power of song to change men and women's lives was an unending topic with Rodeheaver. Although a serious man, he used smiles as a technique to fight for an improved world. Rodeheaver once stated, "I believe there is a worldwide revival of religion coming back.

When it arrives, it will be accomplished through singing gospel songs and teaching others to sing." He further commented, "I go around to the churches and tell people there is no use of sitting there like a lot of sour crab apples, scaring people away! We Christians have a right to be happy." He urged the audience to make a better and brighter place by singing this song:

Do not wait until some deed of greatness you may do,
Do not wait to shed your light afar;
To the many duties ever near you now be true,
Brighten the corner where you are.[11]

Periodical editor Roger Butterfield described Homer Rodeheaver as "a Christian with an old trombone, successfully preaching salvation through song." He further commented on his "smile and rich, mellow voice," saying that "Rody's main asset is his trombone." The trombone "has been seen and heard by more people than any [other] single musical instrument. It is most widely traveled and transported in various countries. Rody has played it standing on top of a stone camel in China, and in the jungles of the Belgian Congo; there the natives called him 'Reverend Trombone.' "[12]

Rodeheaver's Directing of Large and Varied Audiences

During 1936 a chorus of 85,000 people gathered in Chicago's Soldier Field. Huge floodlights shone over the massed faces. This was the finale of

Chicago's summer music festival. Rodeheaver stood on top of a tower of the huge stadium. As he raised his hand, a sudden calm came over the audience.

"Now we'll join in singing the first song," he explained over the public address system. "I'll sing the words while you hum. Everybody!" Instantly the audience began humming as Rody sang the words. From the throats of many thousands, the harmony rose and subsided, drifting into silence. The harmony seemed almost haunting.

After the choral group sang the words, he put the chorus through its paces for three hours. This mastery of audience control and choral singing was evidence of Rody's charisma. The audience could sense his power of persuasion.

His rich baritone voice and trombone had brightened corners in isolated mission stations and in Wanamaker's Philadelphia store. Each year he would travel thousands of miles, appearing at conventions, churches, and state fairs. When radio announcer Lowell Thomas presented Rodeheaver to the New York Advertising Club, Rody eventually had hard-boiled businessmen boisterously singing "Pray the Clouds Away."

Rodeheaver was largely responsible for popularizing the tradition of an annual Easter sunrise service. This practice was first introduced to him at a Moravian church in Winston-Salem, North Carolina. Impressed with this service, he thought, "Why not make this practice universal? Why shouldn't Christians everywhere greet the Easter sun with the music of gratitude and salvation?" The next Easter he directed 2,000 voices on a hillside near Corpus Christi, Texas. Later he continued this practice in Los Angeles, Chicago, Boston, and Philadelphia.[13]

Obstacles and Blessings in the Sunday Campaigns

Billy Sunday was a man devoted to prayer. Frequently he was heard praying while traveling, whether it was by auto or train. Like any other faithful servant of Christ, he was aware of Satan's attack, especially when it involved his own family.

For a while his oldest son George was a member of his staff, and his son Billy Jr. served occasionally as his pianist. Eventually these sons left the campaigns and followed their own way of life. George became an alcoholic and was involved in infidelity. He invested in real estate, where losses brought considerable pressure on him and he committed suicide. Billy Jr. became an alcoholic and lived a very worldly life.

Nell Sunday was involved in an auto accident and had to remain at home a few weeks to recuperate. Their son Paul attended a university and accumulated some debt. All of this pressure, plus the criticisms from the liberal clergy and the press, precipitated Billy Sunday's physical and emotional collapse. He was hospitalized two days in Mayo Clinic and then resumed his preaching ministry.

During 1924 and 1925 his exhausting schedule brought on additional physical problems. Nell Sunday was immobilized with ulcers and had surgery twice at Mayo Clinic. By this time Billy Sunday believed that the obstacles in their ministry came mainly from Satan's attacks. In 1932 their lovely daughter Helen died at the age of 42. This loss was especially difficult since she was so close to her parents.[14]

Unmindful that these various problems were having any effect on his ministry, Sunday continued his endeavors. Eventually Rodeheaver and the staff noticed diminishing attendance. Rodeheaver became aware of complaints from the clergymen and the staff, and he also became the scapegoat of many criticisms. His problems with Sunday began during the early 1920s. Lyle Dorsett mentions a number of these problems. First, Sunday's prancing back and forth on the platform and his obvious fidgeting became most disturbing to the staff. Not only would Sunday sometimes walk around while Rodeheaver and Mrs. Asher were singing, but on occasion he even reached between them to lay his Bible on the pulpit.

Rodeheaver's desire was to render a special song appropriate to Sunday's following message. Rather than being sensitive to Rody's meaningful purpose, Sunday would sometimes crack a joke instead. Naturally this left the impression that Rodeheaver's musical ministry had very little meaning.

Billy Sunday's increased public comments on stinginess in giving in the offerings disturbed both staff and pastors. This was particularly distressing since the audience was much smaller. Occasionally Nell Sunday would attempt to calm the pastors' irritation over her husband's comments. Seemingly the financial stress of his sons caused him to become obsessed with money.

Another major problem was that Sunday's invitational appeals had become rather perplexing. The pastors were especially aware of this. There was uncertainty whether his appeals were to the saved or unsaved. Usually Sunday would plead for repentant sinners to come forward and shake his hand. Rather than making eye contact with the seekers, he would perhaps gaze at the ushers, bawling them out for some oversight. As a result some seekers would return to their seats somewhat bewildered. To Rodeheaver this seemed rude and thoughtless and showed a lack of compassion. Bear in mind that the two men were opposite in personalities: one somewhat belligerent and the other more suave and tactful.[15]

With these various complaints in mind, Rodeheaver wrote a lengthy letter to Nell Sunday, expecting her to share these problems with her husband. Rody was aware that Sunday's wife had more persuasive powers than any of the staff did. Mrs. Sunday temporarily turned down the request, saying that her husband had enough problems on his mind without adding more distress. A few months afterward, Rodeheaver could not see any marked change in his areas of concern. Rodeheaver finally decided that he could not take it any longer. Without any outward display, he left the Sunday organization and bade the staff a warm farewell.[16]

During 1929 Billy Sunday wrote a letter to Rodeheaver, accusing him of ingratitude in regard to all that had been accomplished to make him famous and financially successful. The reference was to Rodeheaver's sale of gospel music from the Rodeheaver Publishing Company, which had been established while Rodeheaver traveled with Sunday. Rody wrote a firm but humble reply saying that he always had held respect for his old partner. He also stated that he had brought up a number of problems, but there had been no change. He further explained that he had written to Nell of certain complaints, but that she had kept them to herself. He referred to the earlier years when Sunday took time to mingle and converse with the pastors, encouraging them and listening to their problems. Once Sunday became a celebrity, he no longer took the time for this communication. Rody also mentioned the low staff morale, mainly because of Sunday's lack of association with the staff. The confident Rodeheaver made his point clear, and his doing so eventually benefited Sunday.

Sometime later during 1931 Rodeheaver wrote to Sunday, "I appreciated the fine virile message. I appreciated also the fine direct invitation you gave." The response to Rodeheaver's letter also revealed excellent progress concerning Sunday's overconcern about money matters. Hollywood had approached Sunday about putting his message on film, and in fact, Rodeheaver was an ally in this offer, mentioning that it would advance his cause and message to a new audience. Sunday, however, had learned his lesson about the enticements of fame, and he declined. During 1933 Billy looked healthy, although his facial features were somewhat sunken. Years of daily preaching, the trials of combating critics, and his having to deal with wavering sons all took their toll.[17]

In 1935 Billy Sunday had a heart attack and was unable to attend the Commencement exercises at Bob Jones College. The doctor of divinity degree he was to receive was given in absentia. After a second heart attack, Sunday preached his last sermon in Mishawaka, Indiana. Afterward the Sundays traveled to Chicago to be with a relative of Nell Sunday. As she was writing a letter, she heard Billy say, "I'm getting dizzy, Ma!" Those were his final words. Rodeheaver sang at his memorial service in Moody Church. The memorial service was planned to challenge God's people in evangelistic work and to bring the lost into the fold. With Dr. Harry Ironside officiating, it did indeed become an evangelistic service.[18]

It should be pointed out that Rodeheaver was not at all desirous of giving a bleak picture of Sunday's final ministry. Indeed, in those years supporting groups for tabernacle ministries were dwindling. In many of the Protestant denominations, personal evangelism was being replaced by a growing emphasis on the social gospel, on Christian education, and on various humanitarian movements. Although Sunday's latter ministry took place in local churches, he never deviated in his preaching method. His mainstay was preaching the gospel and preaching that Christians should forsake sin.

As Rodeheaver states, "He was not dimmed by the shadow of closing days, but emerged more and more clearly into the light." Although men are prone to change during their advancing years, Billy Sunday did not deviate at all from his steady dynamic crusading for Christ. His message remained the same as that of the apostle Paul, who "determined not to know any thing among you, save Jesus Christ, and him crucified" (I Cor. 2:2). To the end, Sunday remained the same energetic, forceful evangelist of righteousness. Rodeheaver stated, "Whenever Sunday gave an invitation, I always wanted to hit the sawdust trail."[19]

Right: *Homer Rodeheaver with the Sundays*

Left: *Rody leading the congregational singing*
Bottom: *From left, Bob Matthews, Mrs. William Asher, Homer Rodeheaver, Mrs. Sunday, and Billy Sunday*

A group of Sunday workers in the Cincinnati campaign

chapter five

Rodeheaver's Contributions

While Homer Rodeheaver was traveling with Billy Sunday, he became involved in the publishing of gospel song books. Over time the Rodeheaver Company grew to be one of the largest publishers of gospel music. Its original name was the Rodeheaver-Ackley Company, a partnership of Homer Rodeheaver and Bentley D. Ackley. Then during 1911 this music publishing enterprise continued in Chicago as the Rodeheaver Company. Also affiliated with the business was Homer's oldest brother, Yumbert. Eventually, the second of the three brothers, Dr. Joseph N. Rodeheaver, joined the staff.

After making considerable progress, the company purchased the Praise Publishing Company of Philadelphia. During the middle 1930s, the Rodeheaver Company invested in the Hall-Mack Company. Even before its 1941 move to Winona

Lake, Indiana, the company established offices in Philadelphia and Chicago. However, with the move to Winona Lake, the company established its administrative center in the Westminster Hotel. In 1948 the western branch office became known as a sales outlet with Paul Moon as overseer.

Over the years the company did well. Joseph Rodeheaver's death occurred in 1946, Yumbert's in 1950, and Homer's in 1955. George W. Sanville, who was associated with the company from 1912 until his death in 1957, played a prominent part in the success of the business. Much of the success of this company is attributed to the fine gospel songwriters of its day. These included Charles N. Gabriel, B. D. Ackley, J. Lincoln Hall, Adam Geibel, C. Austin Miles, George Bennard, A. W. Ackley, Virgil P. Brock, Norman J. Clayton, George S. Schuler, John M. Hallet, and Gloria Roe. After Homer's death, the company came under the management of James E. Thomas, husband of Ruth Rodeheaver Thomas. Meanwhile, N. Bruce Howe Jr. had joined the company in 1941; he became executive vice president and later president. In more recent years, the Rodeheaver Hall-Mack Company has become part of Word Incorporated.

Some of the well-known gospel songs that Rody made famous are "In the Garden," "The Old Rugged Cross," "Beyond the Sunset," "Somebody Cares," "Forgive Me, Lord," "When the World Forgets," and "Goodnight Here and Good Morning Up There." Of course, many others could be named. Many years after Homer's death, these same gospel songs are still prominent and are used by many evangelical religious groups.

Rody was never content unless he could make use of every available means of proclaiming the gospel in song. Consequently, he seized the opportunity of making disks for the phonograph. The Edison phonograph was not operated electrically, but instead a crank started the mechanism in motion. The Edison platters were disks almost a quarter of an inch thick. Later the disks were reduced to an eighth of an inch and played at seventy-eight revolutions per minute. On the Edison records Rody recorded such gospel songs as "Where They Never Say Goodbye" and "Tell Me the Story of Jesus."

During the years that Rodeheaver traveled with Billy Sunday, he produced the Victor Sacred Records. One recording that sold exceedingly well among evangelical Christians contained "Forgive Me, Lord" and "The Old Rugged Cross." It was reported that the Victor recording company sold over a million copies of this one record.

Eventually, the Columbia and Decca recording companies presented a series of soul-searching, heart-warming gospel songs. Decca recorded "A Crown Without a Thorn," "When God Is Near," "Wonderful," "God Understands," "The Glory of His Presence," "You Must Open the Door," "Jesus Took My Burden," and "Heartaches." Ultimately the Rainbow recording company joined the project. In a number of these Rainbow recordings,

I served as organist for Rodeheaver and his sister Ruth. On a Rainbow disk, Rody sang jubilantly a Christmas greeting, "Wishing You a Merry Christmas."[2]

Rainbow Ranch: A Home for Homeless Boys

An unusual host, Rodeheaver was often surrounded by young people. His pleasing magnetism attracted teenagers as well as those of junior age. In fact, Rody's compassion extended to the needs of homeless children, especially boys.

Envisioning a home for such boys, he decided to purchase a thousand feet of ocean frontage between Melbourne Beach and the Sebastian inlet near Palatka, Florida. He also built a large rambling bungalow near the oceanfront. The plot of land was bordered by Rody Drive to the north and Budris Drive on the south. One street was named Winona Road after his summer home in Indiana, and another street was named Casurina, a scientific name for an Australian pine. On opposite sides of the plot were the Atlantic Ocean and the Indian River.

Rody frequently visited the ranch. One would find him singing to the boys and strumming his guitar. It was obvious that the boys thoroughly enjoyed his patter and musical entertainment.

One active service club assisting the boys' ranch was made up of several young men from the Palatka senior high school. They were members of the Interact Club, sponsored by the Palatka Rotary Club. Throughout the year these young men gave their time and money to aid the boys at the ranch. Bob Webb, a member of the Palatka executive board and of the Rotary Club, sought to help guide the young men in their service work. These young men built a half-mile fence and completed it in one day.

The Reverend Lee C. Fisher, my close friend, was director of the ranch for some time. Certainly his services were a real asset and an inspiration to the boys. Again, Rody's vision, his compassion, his finances, and his practical attention will be long remembered.

Top: *Rody singing with boys from Rainbow Ranch*
Bottom: *Editors and compositors from Rodeheaver Publishing Company*

chapter six

Rodeheaver's Charisma and Compassion

Rodeheaver delighted in dwelling on the amiable traits of anyone who desired to succeed. At times his comments would seem like mere flattery, especially in the presence of charming young ladies, and perhaps they were. Nevertheless, Rody delighted in dwelling on the beauty and good of anyone or any group that deserved it. On one occasion Rody's compliments were expressed to a certain evangelist in my presence. This evangelist, having a high-strung, impetuous personality, bluntly remarked, "Rody, don't you ever say anything negative of a person once in a while, rather than give all that applesauce?" I could tell that Rodeheaver was deeply offended by such rudeness. After gaining his composure, he dryly replied in his Southern drawl, "Sir, if you desire that I dwell on the worst within you, I'll be obliged to do so." Soon the evangelist came to his senses and humbly apologized for his rudeness.

I always admired Rody's patience and his sense of humility. Indeed, his patience much exceeded mine. He had the unique ability of making not only his friends but also strangers feel at ease publicly.

The following incident took place during the "platform hour" of the School of Sacred Music. Anyone who offered to sing was permitted to do so. A certain young man volunteered to sing a gospel solo, with his mother as the accompanist. During the rendition the young man became flustered and forgot both the words and the melody of the song.

The young man's mother, frustrated from the ordeal, decided to come to her son's rescue. She chimed in with a shrill high soprano and a nasal twang, singing partially off-key in the higher notes. To be sure, this added to the pandemonium, and to me, this was one of the most hilarious moments of misery I ever experienced. I greatly marveled that Rody could keep his composure throughout this audition.

In his usual mild manner, Rodeheaver made the mother feel at ease by commenting, "Now that is just *like* a mother, ready to come to her son's rescue. After all, what are mothers for?" After these comments, both mother and son felt at ease, as did the student body.

Rodeheaver dearly loved young people, as he demonstrated by sending two Korean brothers through college. One of the boys took the name Rody Hyun and the other Homer Hyun. Rody Hyun possessed a beautiful tenor voice, and he won a prize in a contest with American boys. For several years he taught in one of the missionary schools of South Korea and was also involved in evangelistic work.

Rodeheaver had received a number of instruments that were donated by people throughout the United States for a band and orchestra in Seoul. Rody Hyun's band members would hold evangelistic meetings and sing on the streets. In 1946 it was my privilege to accompany Rody Hyun on the organ as he sang some of the tenor roles in the *Messiah.*[1]

During the platform hour of the School of Music, gospel hymn composer B. D. Ackley was one who never publicly expressed himself. Rodeheaver would occasionally say in jest to the group, "You know, Ackley talks so much that I hardly get a word in edgewise." I once mentioned this to Ackley's daughter, Gertrude Dye. She replied, "Yes, he was quiet then, but my father could say more in one sentence than some preachers could say in two or three paragraphs."

Rodeheaver had his lighter moments, particularly with children. In a large city, he served as Santa Claus in the presence of Eleanor Roosevelt. Franklin D. Roosevelt called Rody "the only authorized Santa during [Roosevelt's] term in office."[2]

His unpredictable antics could not be overlooked. On one occasion at the dinner table, a relative of Jim Thomas made the remark, "Rody, I wish you would catch me a fish while I am here." He immediately jumped up from the table, got his fishing pole, and within a short while caught a good-size bass for the "dear soul."

One day I had gone fishing with my uncle at a nearby lake. Since my sons were with me at the time, we had caught more fish than we could consume. After the fish were cleaned, I gave some to Rodeheaver and his sister, Ruth. They were so appreciative of the fish that one would think I had given them a thousand dollars. Regardless of how small the gift, they always showed gratitude. I have often thought it was the friendship and fellowship they desired the most. With many people, the Rodeheavers were always on the giving end.

It has been reported that Rodeheaver sang himself into the hearts of millions of people. He became nationally known for his ability to make his audience sing. He was the first man to conduct a community sing program on the radio; it was carried by both NBC and CBS. He was called a man of rare personality: singer, speaker, reader, and trombone player. His performances expressed the spirit of friendliness, and they were always entertaining and spiritually helpful. As Rodeheaver's popularity grew, the demands on his time and talents grew. For about two years, he was director of singing at the Canadian National Exhibit.[3]

Will Rogers thought highly of Rodeheaver's persuasiveness as a song leader:

> Rody is the fellow that can make you sing whether you want to or not. I think he has more terrible voices in what was supposed to be unison than any man in the world. Everyone sings for Rody![4]

Rodeheaver's popularity in Winona Lake was greatly enhanced by the entertainment provided by Ruth and her husband Jim. Jim, an elegant and outstanding Virginia businessman, was a vital part of the Rodeheaver music publishing business. This lovely couple served as host and hostess, always gracious in hospitality. As many as thirty-five people from all walks of life—Bible instructors, preachers, opera stars, pastors, and some blue-collar workers—would be gathered around the table on the spacious screened-in porch. Ruth always made it a practice to inquire if anyone had a birthday. If someone did, Ruth would signal for the housemaid, Helen Sellers, to select an appropriate gift for that person.

On one occasion some guests were served on the mansion's flat roof. Evidently there was too much weight on one end, and a corner of the roof caved in. No doubt the problem was readily taken care of in the Thomases' usual gracious manner.

Ruth was an artist of superior talent with a marvelous soprano voice. She often sang solos and duets with Homer. Her voice was well adapted to gospel songs, yet she was also highly proficient in concert and oratorio renditions. She freely sang some of the most difficult passages, always employing meaningful phrasing. Like her brother, Ruth held her audience by her person as well as her performance. Seth Parker once said, "When charming Ruth Thomas gets up to entertain the folks with the sweet olden time songs for which she has a fame all of her own, everyone will know that it is sophisticated only by virtue of a finely trained and beautiful voice."[5]

Rody never married, although he met a few women who had an attraction for him. In fact, one proposal brought on a breach of promise suit. One questions whether he was seriously in love with any woman. Perhaps he was merely in love with the notion of romance itself. His significant amount of traveling and his independent spirit seemingly ruled out the possibility of marriage.[6]

Rodeheaver's Abhorrence of the Liquor Traffic

When the Eighteenth Amendment was repealed, liquor was once again legal in the United States. Rodeheaver strongly abhorred the liquor traffic because of its influence on the youth of America. In a 1947 sermon he recalled that during World War I American soldiers were forbidden to drink liquor in any manner. In England the situation was different: English soldiers drank heavily, being enticed by attractive women servers. Naturally, this situation affected the American soldiers as well. Then under a Democrat administration, liquor began to flow throughout the United States and in the military camps.

During World War II, military officers were allowed to disburse liquor in their clubs. Brewers announced, "This is the greatest opportunity ever given to the brewing industry." As Rodeheaver stated, "Hell howled with glee; the devil, the brewers, and the saloon keepers laughed and raked in the profits." He further stated, "Mothers wept over boys who went out with great patriotic zeal and came home drunkards." No pension and no benefits can ever dry the tears of broken-hearted mothers. Only the preaching of the gospel and the saving grace of Jesus Christ can transform such lives.

Rodeheaver pled nationwide for the churches to show more responsibility in this matter, and he even urged the Winona Lake Christian Assembly to take this matter in hand. He encouraged Christian people to get involved in some Christian temperance society. He placed his sanction on a tract for youth: "You can—say no! Thank you." The tract, urging youth not to sacrifice principle for popularity, cited abstainers such as Henry Ford, Thomas A. Edison, Luther Burbank, and Roger Babson.[7]

Likewise, Billy Sunday strongly denounced the use of alcohol and believed that its use was Satanic. In Sunday's earlier ministry, he gave much emphasis to personal salvation. After 1907 he preached sermons against the saloons such as "Get on the Water Wagon." Sunday began to give more emphasis to delivering American cities from a variety of sinful practices. Even though Billy and Nell Sunday frequently mingled with the social and political elite, they never neglected their visits to the rescue missions and the jails where Billy preached the gospel. By the end of 1917, thousands had "hit the sawdust trail"—over 64,000 in Boston and 98,269 in New York.[8]

Rodeheaver's Enjoyment of Entertainment and Sports

Rodeheaver enjoyed participating in a variety of sports. Since he lived at Winona Lake much of his life, he particularly enjoyed the water. During the Rodeheaver School of Music, he would frequently take some of his friends out on the lake in his motorboat. Rody enjoyed water-skiing on a homemade toboggan or using the sliding board that went from his bedroom down to the lake. However, the slide became so popular that visitors would come by to see it and would occasionally request to use it. Eventually, this situation became so burdensome that he had the slide taken down.

Rody loved baseball, but he participated in it very little. However, he did speak fondly of one game as a game to remember. With Rodeheaver as the catcher, Douglas Fairbanks Jr. as the batter, and Billy Sunday as the pitcher, the three decided to have their picture taken while playing softball. Their smiles showed that they were thoroughly enjoying themselves.

The Westminster Hotel, headquarters for the Rodeheaver School of Sacred Music, had many recreational features, including bowling alleys and table tennis. Taking into account the water activities at the lake such as swimming and ferryboat rides, no member seemed to lack for something to do.

The participants in the school of music would frequently gather in the Rainbow Room of the Westminster Hotel. During the platform hour, Rody took delight in having different drama teams perform a skit. At times he would even participate. The school of music was not only a time of instruction and learning, but also a time of entertainment and relaxation.

Rodeheaver loved to travel, and he would frequently take off in his 1924 Chrysler. He had a propensity for doing the unusual, spontaneous thing. While visiting Palestine, the party went to the Dead Sea. While there, he had an urge to float in the buoyant, salty waters of the Dead Sea. Not only did he take a dip in the water, but, floating with trombone in hand, he played his usual song, "Brighten the Corner."[9]

Top: *Eleanor Roosevelt with Rody as Santa*
Bottom: *Rodeheaver, Douglas Fairbanks Jr., and Billy Sunday playing "a game to remember"*

Top: *Rody water-skiing on his homemade toboggan*
Bottom: *Fun on Winona Lake*

chapter seven

The Rodeheaver School of Sacred Music

The Origin of the School of Sacred Music

While Rodeheaver was with Billy Sunday, many pastors inquired about where young leaders in the churches could receive training in vocal work and musical leadership. In response to these inquiries, Rodeheaver organized a short musical training school to be held each August in connection with the annual Bible conference at Winona Lake, Indiana. To this religious training school he brought the finest voice teachers of America. After his death in 1955, the school continued its services until the late 1960s.

During the 1930s through the 1950s, many evangelists attended the Bible conference with the intent of making contacts with potential singers, music conductors, and pianists. In 1935 I made such a contact with evangelist G. E. Vinaroff, a naturalized U.S. citizen from Macedonia. I traveled with him for three years as his pianist, youth worker, and children's worker. Many other young men were fortunate to make a similar contact with an evangelist or pastor with whom they eventually served.

Rodeheaver told of a handsome young farm boy who worked on a dairy farm near Winona Lake. The boy's job was to milk the cows and deliver the milk to the customers nearby. He had a beautiful voice and had the potential of using it for the Lord. Rodeheaver suggested that he attend the music conference to receive some instruction with the possibility of becoming an evangelistic singer and song leader.

The young man said, "I've got to milk the cows." Rodeheaver persisted, telling him to get a substitute and find out what some musical training would do for him. He did so. During the second year he was introduced to an evangelist. The young man left the farm and traveled with this evangelist for four years.

The young man then settled in Grove City, Pennsylvania, because of his growing family. Eventually he became one of the leading men of the Kiwanis Club, both locally and nationally. He was part of the committee that compiled the songbook for the Kiwanis Club. After some years, he moved to Detroit and became the minister of music in a Presbyterian church. His activities were further extended as the educational director for children. He served in this church for several years. He would return for an occasional visit to the old farm near Winona and would preach or sing in various churches in that area.[1]

Those who were later called to military service found the sacred music course most valuable to assist with group singing in the military.

At the School of Sacred Music there was a general conference hour to which various ministers were invited. They were asked to give criticism of, and suggestions for, singers who had made their meetings difficult. It was a general open forum in which pupils were presented for observation, and constructive criticism was requested from the audience. In turn, the singers were given an opportunity to say what was on their mind concerning some preachers with whom they had been associated. Certainly such discussions were most interesting.[2]

The Music Faculty of the School of Sacred Music

Supervising the entire school himself, Rodeheaver always assembled an outstanding music faculty. The following served there during the 1940s.

Rollin Pease, head of the voice department at Arizona University, was an outstanding voice teacher and one who sang the part of Elijah in the oratorio *Elijah*. Griffith Jones, head of music in the Cleveland public schools for thirty years, was one of the greatest authorities on children's voices. Director of the women's chorus at the School of Music, Jones would occasionally have the women sing "The Holy City" with a children's descant. Katherine Carmichael, a prominent organist, was music director at Third Baptist Church in St. Louis. Ruth Thomas, concert and radio vocalist, was instructor of voice and platform decorum.

Dr. Joseph N. Rodeheaver, with years of experience in education, was dean and student advisor. B. D. Ackley was a well-known gospel songwriter. Clyde L. Wolford, tenor soloist, was a magnetic leader and teacher of song leadership. Louise Taylor was an eminent contralto soloist and voice teacher from Ohio. Mildred Essig, contralto soloist from Warsaw, Indiana, frequently sang from the *Messiah*. During the School of Music, band concerts were a real treat. James Boersma gave instrumental instruction and did orchestral conducting.

Walter Jenkins of Houston directed the men's chorus. Jenkins directed the music in one of the large choirs of that city and was well known as the official song leader for Rotary International. His wife, Vivien, was an outstanding vocalist. I was the organist for the Rodeheaver School of Music. On one occasion the faculty was invited to a church to participate in our four fifty-thousand-watt broadcasting stations' "Back Home Hour" performance.

The Purpose of the Rodeheaver School of Sacred Music

In its early beginning, the Rodeheaver School of Music was sponsored by DePauw University, granting credit for music majors. Later it became an independent organization under Rodeheaver's sponsorship. During the 1930s and 1940s, it was in session for two weeks; during the 1950s and 1960s, it was in session for one week each year.

Its purpose was to stimulate the interest of Christian laymen in developing their performance in some local church. The areas of study were choral conducting, vocal solo work, instrumental performance, organ and piano instruction, hymn accompanying and improvisation, and speech and platform decorum.

The Daily Schedule of the School of Sacred Music

In the 1940s, the time of instruction was typically organized as follows:

A. The forenoon period

1. Get-acquainted day (occasional comments on the aim and purpose of the school)
2. A vocal exercise rehearsal
3. Certain choral numbers introduced for final performance
4. Groups divided into voice range

B. Morning sectional instruction

1. Instrumental (by Mr. Boersma)

2. Organ and piano (by Katherine Carmichael)
3. Platform decorum (by Ruth Thomas)
4. Voice (by Howard Jenkins, Rollin Pease, and Ella Steele)

C. The afternoon period
1. Men's chorus rehearsal (by Clyde Wolford)
2. Women's chorus rehearsal (by Griffith Jones)

D. The platform hour (entire school assemblage)
1. Vocal soloists, women's trios, and men's quartets would perform before the whole school for Rodeheaver's evaluation. He would comment on good points and weaknesses needing improvement. (This took place in the Rainbow Room of the Westminster Hotel.)
2. Rodeheaver would give some informal remarks, quoting one of his poems from *More Worthwhile Poems*. Occasionally he would choose a faculty member or a layman who excelled in speech and platform decorum to recite one of his poems.

E. Frequent sectional choral rehearsals
1. Sometimes the entire student body would dramatize certain oratorios, such as Elijah, with choral background.
2. Other great works were also presented, such as the *Messiah*, the *Redemption*, and "The Holy City," with Katherine Carmichael and me accompanying.

Rodeheaver's Controversy with Conference Coworkers

A controversy arose over Seventh-Day Adventists' enrollment in the School of Sacred Music, and particularly over the performance of a Seventh-Day Adventist quartet during an evening service. Rodeheaver was not very well versed in theology, and because of his past association with certain SDA officials he thought they were soundly evangelical. The confusion took place because of the existence of two groups: the traditional Seventh-Day Adventists and a more exclusive biblical group. The traditional group accepts Ellen White's interpretation and visions as equally inspired as Scripture itself. Thus evangelicals classify it as a cult.

In the 1950s Dr. Donald Grey Barnhouse was ready to accept them as evangelical. While he was giving recognition to Seventh-Day Adventists, one of their leaders was excommunicated (in Australia) for refusing to recognize Ellen White's interpretations. As Edmund C. Gruss expresses it, "In theory they exalt the Bible above the writings of Mrs. White. In practice they do the exact opposite." One major fallacy is Mrs. White's prophecy that no one can have assurance of salvation until the day of judgment. Evangelicals who read their comments about salvation, Scripture, and the Trinity are apt to think of Seventh-Day Adventists as truly evangelical. However, those who dwell upon their peculiar doctrines may question whether they are truly Christian. If theologians have been confused about SDA doctrine, it is not surprising that Rodeheaver, not being a theologian, was confused as well.

When the controversy arose, Rodeheaver declared he was not going to announce that anyone was invited to the School of Sacred Music except for Seventh-Day Adventists. Obviously, his human compassion surpassed his good judgment theologically. However, it should be remembered that his everyday living did indeed express the Christian compassion that all believers should practice.[3]

Rodeheaver School of Sacred Music, 1946

chapter eight

Rodeheaver's Philosophy of Sacred Music

Rodeheaver's philosophy dwelt on the practical aspects of song leadership from his own experience. Song leading is quite simple after a person has a few basic details thoroughly mastered. The hand or baton indicates the different kinds of tempo: 4/4 time requires down, left, right, up; and for 3/4 time the motions are down, right, up. In all time signatures, the accent is normally on the downbeat unless there is syncopation.

When the director has these basic motions fixed in his mind, then he can eventually inject his own personality into the basic design. If the director has the correct rhythmical feel, allowing his arm to come down on the accented beat, he can usually get a good response from the audience. As the director grows in experience, he can begin to interpret the song with hand movement. Hands actually are more expressive than a baton.

Rodeheaver realized that the personal appearance of a director is important—not handsomeness or beauty, but his being well groomed and dressed appropriately. A man's clean clothes, properly tied necktie, and clean-shaven face are real assets in making a good impression upon an audience. He should use good judgment, avoiding anything that would look foolish or distract the audience.

An important function of the director is to create an atmosphere that holds the audience's attention. Any nervous motions on the part of the director will make the audience uneasy. If some commotion is created in the audience, the director's influence is crucial. At that moment he can use smooth hand movements to attract the crowd's attention to himself and express an air of calmness.

A leader needs to strive for an easy manner and cultivate graciousness for the benefit of his audience. Both the song leader and the soloist should concentrate their attention near the center back row of the auditorium, thus appearing to give personal attention to all those in between. If there should be any disruption caused by crying infants, usually the ushers are instructed to take the mother and infant to a back room. Should ushers fail to do so, thoughtful song leaders have been known to slip off the platform and help the mother out of the meeting.

A versatile accompanist is of great importance to a song service or for choral accompanying. An accompanist can either support or destroy good directing. The pianist who has his own ideas of tempo and will not be guided by a director is himself an irritating problem. On one occasion during the Rodeheaver School of Music, the organist expressed her contempt for the fast speed at which the director was conducting the "Hallelujah Chorus." She definitely made it known by playing some staccato tones on the black keys. (She knew that if Rodeheaver were directing, he would prefer the slower tempo.) Although the director may be wrong in his ideas, the accompanist is expected to follow his direction. Such willingness demonstrates the accompanist's ability more than his persistence in flaunting his own ideas.

Rodeheaver felt that the accompanist's introduction for a song is an important matter. The introduction, which should consist of the first four or more measures of the song, has three objectives. It gives the pitch of the song, it sets the tempo and rhythm, and it gives at least the beginning of the tune (an important matter for those who do not read music). A good introduction requires much forethought. One disheartening habit of some pianists is to end on a dominant chord rather than resolving back to the beginning (tonic) chord. Without the beginning chord, the director and audience are left dangling, and it is most difficult for the director to get a good, spontaneous attack from the congregation.

Some accompanists will attempt to be spectacular by over-embellishing the songs, such as flipping off high notes at the close of a stanza. This practice ruins the dignity of many hymns. When the accompanist plays for a worship service, there should be less improvisation. For a gospel song, more freeness of improvisation is acceptable. The lyrics of a song determine what is appropriate as much as do the music and rhythm.

The value of a correct tempo is evident. Any hymn or gospel song can lose its effectiveness if it is sung too fast or too slow. A happy medium will allow the congregation to get the message of the song. One gospel song that is frequently spoiled is "Since Jesus Came into My Heart." Although it is a testimony song, singing it too fast makes it sound frivolous. With its slight syncopation, it can approach the jazzy stage. Other gospel songs that sound ridiculous when sung too fast are "Praise Him! Praise Him!" and "Anywhere with Jesus." Probably any gospel song that consists of consecutive eighth notes would require a moderate tempo to be sung intelligently.

The use of the hands is also important. The leader can use certain little motions to indicate his wishes to a congregation or choir. Wiggling one's fingers can signal that the passage is to be sung softly. For a louder strain, the director should close his hand and beat the dynamics more vigorously. The beginning and closing of the song should be handled well. The director should get the attention of the audience during the playing of the introduction. He should hold up his hands and make a slight hand motion before coming to the actual beginning note, whether on an upbeat or a downbeat.

Rodeheaver also suggested that for a rest or long note it is better to hold the hand still during a holding part and beat the time through for the movement. When the leader conducts a song in which one part holds and the other parts move, he can hold one hand still for the holding part, while the other hand beats out the rhythm for the moving parts. As a conductor becomes more confident, he will feel more at ease in his direction of the song.

An amateur conductor may soon find that constant singing with the audience during song leading can hinder his solo singing. A strenuous and joyous song service could easily affect his voice. When Rodeheaver was traveling with Billy Sunday, he realized that he had to face this problem. In working with a large congregation of fifteen thousand people, he was determined to allow the congregation to do most of the singing. Not having an amplifying system then, he had to exercise discernment about when to use his voice.[1]

The Essentials of Effective Song Leading

Rodeheaver applied the following basics of song leadership both in the pulpit and in the instruction of sacred music. They are important for any student of sacred music.

1. *Sincerity*. To demonstrate sincerity, the song leader must regard service above self. His objective should never be to be seen or heard. His speech

should be friendly, not clever. His purpose should be to seek his audience's enjoyment.

2. *Friendliness.* The song leader should demonstrate a genuine love for people. He should seek a common ground of friendliness with his people.

3. *Confidence.* The leader must have confidence and poise in his approach and technique. He must be able to cope with unexpected situations and to say and do the correct thing during an emergency.

4. *Vitality.* An emotional leader may exaggerate at times, but he must learn control. Song leading calls for strength and magnetism, yet a reservation of power.

5. A *musical ear.* Song leaders are expected to have accurate pitch, good musical taste, and a singing voice with good volume and range.

6. *Good rhythm.* The leader must be able to put the "lift" of good rhythm and tempo into congregational singing.

7. *Flexibility.* He should strive for conformity yet know what is needed in case of an unexpected situation. Sudden changes may call for a change in the program.

8. *Sense of humor.* The song leader should show good sportsmanship and be able to laugh when the joke is on him.

9. *Effective body use.* The leader should possess dynamic poise, not being tense but having a firm posture. A slouchy posture is incompatible with

effective song leadership. He should also avoid extreme motions that would give the impression of a ballet dancer.

10. A *good speaking voice*. A strong speaking voice is a great asset to a leader. The voice should be firm, well pitched, and resonant. His speaking voice is vital in expressing his personality.

11. *Clear enunciation*. The song leader should give importance to vowel sounds and also make good use of the tongue and lips to pronounce consonants clearly. He should avoid running words together but should finish each word before moving on to the next.[2]

Hymns Versus Gospel Songs

Some have wondered about the differences between hymns and gospel songs. Rodeheaver quotes John Greenfield, a Moravian evangelist:

> The hymn is addressed to God. The gospel song is addressed to the people. The hymn is for praise, worship, adoration, and prayer. The gospel song, directed to the people, is to warn them of the consequences of sin [and] to give the promise of liberty, peace, joy, and heaven. Through hymns we may confess our sins to God, claim His mercy and promises, and pledge our loyalty and faithful service. Through the gospel song we can appeal directly to people to do this same thing.[3]

Any evangelistic church feels compelled to use the gospel song. In general, the hymns are primarily used in a formal worship service such as on Sunday morning. Then both gospel songs and hymns are used in the evening service. Gospel songs are generally used in young people's services and in the Sunday school. Some gospel songs and choruses sound trifling, so one must use good judgment. There are many fine Christians who have never realized the joy of their salvation. Many of the great revivals in the days of Finney, Moody, Sankey, and Sunday proved successful with the help of the gospel song.

As a word of personal testimony, it was through the ministry of a gospel song that I came to know the Lord as my personal Savior. The evangelist's son, Lee C. Fisher, sang the gospel song "For I Was a Sinner, but Christ Made Me Whole." While lying in bed that night, I found myself crying. At first I did not know why I was crying, yet the words of that song kept going through my mind. As a fourteen-year-old boy, I came to realize that I was a sinner. That night I confessed my sins and claimed Christ as my Lord and Savior.

chapter nine

Rodeheaver's Final Days

Roland Felts met Homer Rodeheaver during the summer of 1951. After finishing college, he joined the Rodeheaver Publishing Company as an associate music director. Mr. Felts recalled one incident that was most baffling to Rody—one that Rodeheaver never fully overcame. It happened on a very cold day in February of 1952. Felts and Rodeheaver were in Vandalia, Illinois, for a meeting in a Methodist church with Clovis Chappell. They went out for dinner with the pastor and some other friends. Since they were to return for the evening service, Rodeheaver decided to leave his trombone under the piano. When they returned from dinner, the trombone was missing, and it was never found.

This was a great loss to Rodeheaver. Not only was this the trombone that had gone around the world with him several times, but it was the only trombone he felt comfortable using. The Conn Company of Elkhart, Indiana, had previously presented him with a new trombone. Rody had tried to use it, but the bell was too large and the positions were different. Now he took it up again, but his playing was never the same. As a result, he more often held the new trombone over his shoulder, rather than actually using it. His appearance on the platform was not the same as before.

During the early 1950s, Rodeheaver had a mild heart attack. In various social and church gatherings, he was frequently called on to play his trombone. Aware of the possible strain on his heart from the trombone performance, he would wonder why he was not called on to sing instead. One afternoon a businessman came to visit Rody in his bedroom. The gentleman was so impressed with his visit that he came downstairs saying, "You know, that man is indestructible!" Shortly afterward, a nurse came downstairs to announce that Rodeheaver had passed away.

Rodeheaver died on December 18, 1955; he was 75 years old. His memorial service was conducted in the Methodist church of Warsaw, Indiana, and his body was interred in the Rodeheaver plot nearby. As one of Rodeheaver's songs expresses, "When we step from this earth to God's heaven so fair, / We'll say 'good night' here, but 'good morning' up there."

Homer Rodeheaver was a man who loved his Lord and a man who loved people. He expressed his love of God in his singing, and he humbly expressed his love for people in deeds of kindness. Four words describe Rodeheaver's life: spirituality, charisma, humility, and compassion.

Rodeheaver's compassion is well expressed in the following poem:

A Little Prayer

If any little word of mine
  May make a life the brighter;
If any little song of mine
  May make a heart the lighter,
God help me speak the little word,
  And take my bit of singing,
And drop it in some lonely vale
  To set the echoes ringing.

If any little love of mine
  May make a life the sweeter;
If any little care of mine
  May make a friend's the fleeter;
If any little lift may ease
  The burden of another,
God give me love, and care and
  strength
  To help my toiling brother[1].

This poem truly expresses the heart of my friend, Homer Rodeheaver.

Top: *Homer Rodeheaver*
Left: *Rodeheaver directing at Bob Jones University*

. Bob Jones Jr. and Homer Rodeheaver in front of Rodeheaver Auditorium, Bob Jones University

chapter ten

Stories of Gospel Hymns and Composers

This section tells about gospel hymns and composers that have been directly or indirectly associated with the Rodeheaver Hall-Mack Company. These sketches combine to give a fuller picture of the era of Homer Rodeheaver.

A. H. and B. D. Ackley

The Ackley name is prominent in almost every evangelical hymnal that includes gospel songs. The Ackleys were known for such songs as "I Walk with the King," "God's Tomorrow," "Take Up Thy Cross and Follow Me," and "Mother's Prayers Have Followed Me." The Ackleys' father, a Methodist, was known for his musical abilities. B. D. Ackley, the eldest son, was Billy Sunday's pianist and secretary for a while. B. D. traveled with Rodeheaver as the pianist while also serving as a music editor for the Rodeheaver Company. B. D. Ackley frequently referred to Charles A. Gabriel Jr. as his main source of musical inspiration in gospel hymn writing. B. D.'s home was in Philadelphia, but he spent his last days in Winona Lake, Indiana. He died in September of 1958 and was buried in Oakwood Cemetery.

Alfred H. Ackley was born in Pennsylvania, where he received musical training under excellent teachers and concentrated on the study of the cello. He became first cellist in a prominent orchestra. Later he entered the ministry and received Presbyterian ordination. Although he made his home in Los Angeles, he would frequently visit the home office of the Rodeheaver Company in Winona Lake, Indiana.

The brothers collaborated on the writing of such gospel songs as "In the Service of the King," "Jesus, I Am Coming Home Today," and "Somebody Knows."

"Somebody Knows" was the first song that the Ackleys co-authored. A. H. and his brother were walking down the street in a Pennsylvania town. B. D. was pondering some bad news he had just received. Suddenly he turned to A. H. and said, "Isn't it encouraging that *Somebody knows?*" Immediately they decided that the phrase would make a wonderful theme for a song. When they came upon a music store, they requested that they might use a piano. Shortly the song was completed just as it remains today. Its widespread use was an encouragement to write additional Christian songs.

A. H. Ackley himself later wrote a number of gospel songs, both words and music. Examples are "He Lives" and "Heartaches."

B. D. Ackley also collaborated with many other hymn writers; they would write the words and B. D. would write the music. These include "I Walk with the King" and "I Would Be Like Jesus," words by James Rowe; "Joy in Serving Jesus," words by Oswald J. Smith; and "Mother's Prayers Have Followed Me," words by Lizzie DeArmond.[1]

Virgil and Blanche Kerr Brock

During a revival service in 1918, the Brocks heard an inspirational testimony from a Christian businessman who was a member of Gideons International. During the testimony his constant repetition of the sentence "Oh, He's a wonderful Savior to me" compelled the Brocks to write a gospel song with that theme in mind. It became one of the favorite revival songs.

Blanche Kerr became prominent in Christian service during her youth, playing and singing in evangelistic campaigns. After a brief period of teaching school, she acquired musical training in Indianapolis and Chicago. Later she married Virgil Brock, whom she had met in college. They continued in their work of evangelism, preaching, playing, singing, and writing gospel songs.

In 1936 the Brocks wrote "Beyond the Sunset" after being inspired by the beautiful sunset they observed from Rodeheaver's home. At that time the Brocks were assisting Rodeheaver in his school of music. This song became increasingly popular.

Although their home was in Indianapolis, they had a combination summer home and restaurant in the back of the Billy Sunday Tabernacle. Occasionally Mr. Brock could be heard singing. Some time after his first wife's death, Virgil Brock remarried. He would often say, "My first wife knew how to *play*, but my second wife knows how to *pray*." After his death, a tombstone was erected in Oakwood Cemetery, having engraved on it the music and lyrics of "Beyond the Sunset."[2]

George Bennard

During 1913 George Bennard wrote "The Old Rugged Cross" while in Michigan. The theme of the cross first impressed him, and later he wrote the melody. However, it was not until he had a personal testing of his faith that he completed the words. He first sang the song while he was visiting in Pokagon, Michigan, with his friends Reverend and Mrs. L. O. Bostwick. They were so impressed with the song that they immediately offered to pay him for the first printed copy. The song was performed soon afterward at a large Chicago convention. From that time on, its popularity exceeded that of all other secular or religious songs.

George Bennard was born on February 4, 1873, in Youngstown, Ohio. At first Bennard worked with the Salvation Army, and later he was ordained as a Methodist preacher. He died on October 9, 1958. Bennard's other compositions include such favorites as "Jesus Is Dearer Than All" and "Speak, My Lord."[3]

Charles H. Gabriel

Charles Gabriel was the composer of "The Way of the Cross Leads Home," "Since Jesus Came into My Heart," and "Oh, That Will Be Glory for Me."

Charles was born in Iowa on August 18, 1856. In the prairie settlement where he lived, the settlers often gathered for singing sessions. Charles' father often served as the leader. The boy became most fond of music, and he eventually developed a gift for composing. He told his mother that one day he would write a song that would become famous. She responded, "My boy, I would rather have you write a song that will help somebody, than see you President of the United States."

Charles didn't see his first piano until the age of fourteen, after his family had purchased a small reed organ. He organized a village band and wrote a number of band arrangements that later were published and widely used. On one occasion he supplied words and music for almost seventy pages of a songbook. One hundred copies were sold; he received no remuneration, but instead he received three dozen copies of the book. In that early period he sold many of his songs, but he seldom received more than two and a half dollars for a song.

Later Gabriel began traveling, giving instruction in singing schools, and taking charge of musical conventions. He served as music director of a church in San Francisco. In 1892 he settled in Chicago and became associated with various publishers, including the Rodeheaver Company. Because many of his songs were rejected, he published them himself. They include "The Way of the Cross Leads Home," "He Is So Precious to Me," and "He Lifted Me." In time, all of his productions were in demand.

Charles Gabriel edited thirty-five gospel songbooks, seven books for male voices, a book of children's songs, forty-one Christmas cantatas, several children's cantatas, and some instruction books. During this productive period Charles Gabriel and B. D. Ackley became acquainted. Gabriel died in Berkeley, California, on September 14, 1932.[4]

C. Austin Miles

C. Austin Miles was born on January 7, 1868, in Lakehurst, New Jersey. His musical career began at the age of twelve when he was invited to play for a funeral in a local Methodist church. He was asked to play a slow march while the mourners viewed the departed. The boy played the only slow march he knew. The preacher and the mourners thanked him for his comforting music, and his mother gleamed with pride. Five years later he found out that the slow march he had played for the funeral was Lohengrin's Wedding March.

In 1912 Dr. Adam Geibel requested that Miles write a hymn poem that would evoke sympathy, breathing tenderness in every line. When the verses were completed, Dr. Geibel tried in vain to write a melody for them. He returned the poem to Miles, believing Miles could accomplish something with it. In writing the words and later the music, Miles meditated on a biblical garden scene.

Out of this scene at early dawn comes a woman's form, tearful, hesitating, seeking, and turning from side to side in bewilderment. Finally she whispers, "If thou hast borne him hence. . . ." Then "He speaks, and the sound of His voice is so sweet the birds hush their singing." Jesus says to her, "Mary." Just one word from His lips and all heartache is forgotten—the past blotted out; grief and tears gone; sin, death, and hell no longer to dread. "And the joy we share as we tarry there, none other has ever known." The song "In the Garden" became one of the best-loved gospel songs of all time, second only to "The Old Rugged Cross."

Austin Miles wrote his first gospel song at the age of twenty-five. Later he left his profession in pharmacy and joined the Hall-Mack Publishing Company. He served as manager of this company for twenty-five years. Miles had been with the company forty-three years when it became the Rodeheaver Hall-Mack Company. Miles had written "Dwelling in Beulah Land" and "If Jesus Goes with Me, I'll Go." C. Austin Miles retired in 1942 and died on March 10, 1946, in Pitman, New Jersey.[5]

Lizzie DeArmond

Lizzie DeArmond, of Pennsylvania, was grieving the death of her daughter. During her grief she seemed to be conscious of the Lord speaking to her: "[As] surely as you said 'good night' here to your daughter, you will be saying 'good morning' up there after a while." As a result she wrote a poem which was later set to music by Homer Rodeheaver. Rodeheaver sang "Good Night and Good Morning" sometime later at Mrs. DeArmond's and Billy Sunday's memorial services. Strangely enough, it was also one of the two songs sung at the funeral of the notorious gangster John Dillinger.[6]

Mrs. Edward Augsburger

Mr. and Mrs. Edward Augsburger and family lived in Ft. Wayne, Indiana. They operated a butcher shop and lived a humble, dedicated life in their service and testimony to the Lord. Mrs. Augsburger, a close friend of ours, had an unassuming personality. She and her husband were members of the Ft. Wayne Gospel Temple, where they faithfully sang in the choir.

Mrs. Augsburger had written the song "My Prayer" and had received a copyright in 1936 through the Rodeheaver Company. Rodeheaver and his sister, Ruth, frequently sang this song as a duet. One of our choir members introduced Mrs. Augsburger to Rodeheaver and found that this was their first meeting. The Augsburgers' son, one of the leading youths in our young people's society, later became president of a Baptist college.

Fannie Edna Stafford

Fannie Edna Stafford, who was a semi-invalid for many years, was prone to give in to discouragement. In one very dark hour, the Lord made Himself known to her and gave her peace and comfort. As a result she was inspired to write "Somebody Cares."

Although she lacked courage, Fannie Edna Stafford finally sent the poem to Rodeheaver written on a postcard. She had never met Rodeheaver. No doubt the music he wrote for her poem was a happy surprise for her. This song was one of his first attempts at composition. Certainly the song became a blessing to numerous Christians throughout America.[7]

Lida Shivers Leech and Adam Geibel

The husband of Adam Geibel's only daughter was burned to death in an explosion at the steel mill where he was a foreman. The couple had recently been married, and the young man was an earnest Christian. Sometime later Geibel visited his friend, C. Austin Miles, and told of having been lying in bed meditating on his sorrow and on his daughter's deep distress.

Geibel said, "I heard a voice say to me, 'Child, you do not understand now, but some day it all will be made plain.'" Geibel cried out, "Yes, Lord, I believe; help Thou mine unbelief! I know Thou wilt make it plain to me some day."

He wrote down the melody and a rough idea of the lyrics he wanted. He sent these to Lida Shivers Leech. After her third attempt, the poem satisfied Dr. Geibel.

Dr. Geibel was born in Germany in 1885, and as a child he came to America with his family in his early childhood. He became a teacher, an organist, a conductor, and a composer. He headed the Geibel Music Company, which eventually united with the Rodeheaver Company.

Mrs. Leech did not begin writing poetry until she had passed the age of thirty-five. The Hall-Mack Company was her first publisher. In later life, Mrs. Leech moved from Merchantville, New Jersey, to Hollywood, California, to live with her son. More than five hundred of her songs were published. The best known ones are "Some Day He'll Make It Plain" and "God's Way Is the Best Way."[8]

Oswald J. Smith

Oswald J. Smith was a man of many gifts. He was a pastor, a hymn writer, a missionary statesman, and an evangelist. He was born in 1890, and from early childhood he felt he would be a minister. He took classes at Toronto Bible College and graduated from McCormick Theological Seminary. Although he had an interest in missions, uncertain health kept him from overseas missionary service.

Twenty-two years after he was converted in the Cosmopolitan Tabernacle in Toronto, Canada, he was called to be its pastor, and it became the People's Church. His major emphasis throughout his lifetime was evangelism and the support of global missions. His contributions as pastor, church builder, and missionary statesman were outstanding.

However, Oswald J. Smith was best known as a gospel hymn writer. Some of his most familiar gospel hymns are "Song of the Soul Set Free," "The Glory of His Presence," "Deeper and Deeper," "He Rose Triumphantly," and "Then Jesus Came." Most of these gospel songs were published by the Rodeheaver Publishing Company. Rodeheaver took delight in singing "Then Jesus Came," most often by request. He would usually speak the leper's response "Unclean! Unclean!" rather than singing it.

Oswald J. Smith died in 1986 at the age of 96. He was "obsessed" and "possessed" with getting "every soul to Christ."[9]

Harry A. Ironside

Harry Ironside was not formally ordained, yet he was considered the unofficial archbishop of

Christian Fundamentalism. He had no classroom education beyond elementary school, yet he was regarded as one of the outstanding Bible scholars of his generation. He received an honorary doctorate of literature from the largest liberal arts college in Illinois. He wrote more than forty widely sold books and commentaries. He also wrote the lyrics of one well-loved gospel song, "Overshadowed," assigned to the Rodeheaver Publishing Company. George S. Schuler wrote the music.

Ironside's father died when Harry was only two years old. His mother earnestly prayed that Harry would live for the Lord. On one occasion Harry heard that D. L. Moody was in Los Angeles to speak. Hazzard's Pavilion had no seat for him, but he pushed his way into the balcony. Noticing that large plank girders supported the roof, he climbed up the slanting trough and found a spot from which he could look down on the platform and see everything. He never forgot the forceful preaching of Moody and the singing of George Stebbins that night.

One day when he was fourteen, he came under deep conviction while attending a party. He ran home and accepted Christ as his Savior. Soon afterward the spirit and activity of the Salvation Army attracted him. He longed for the spirit of complete holiness and eradication of sin. In discussing the matter with an older woman, he found that she too had experiential doubts of eradication. Soon they realized from the Scripture that they had everything in Christ, not in an experience.

Having no denominational affiliation, Ironside preached on street corners and in missions. At twenty-three, he married Helen Scofield, daughter of a Presbyterian preacher. Eventually he became affiliated with the Plymouth Brethren. Doctrinally, he accepted a mild form of Calvinism. In 1929 Dr. P. W. Philpott resigned the pastorate of Moody Church. Other preachers such as D. L. Moody, A. C. Dixon, R. A. Torrey, J. M. Gray, and Paul Rader had presided there. Finally in 1930 the church leaders called the fifty-three-year-old Brethren evangelist, who had never before held a pastorate or been ordained. After some discussion with the Plymouth Brethren, Ironside accepted the pastorate of Moody Church. During his fourteen years as pastor, over four thousand parishioners attended his services.

In Ironside's advancing years, his eyesight became dim. However, his memory of Scripture and events compensated for his weakened eyesight. Because of his outstanding published works, Ironside is better known as an author rather than a preacher. In the Lord's work, he was less concerned with organization than with individual consecration.[10]

Haldor and Bertha Mae Lillenas

In 1885 Haldor Lillenas was born in Norway and was later brought to America. He lived on a South Dakota farm for a short while, and then his family moved to Oregon. As a young man, he decided on a career as a chemist. At the age of twenty he was converted and felt a call to the ministry.

Having an outstanding musical talent, Lillenas took musical training from excellent teachers in Chicago and finally received the Doctor of Music degree. He also took theological training and entered the ministry in the Nazarene denomination. For a number of years he served as pastor and evangelist.

Eventually Lillenas decided to devote his entire time to the writing and publishing of Christian music. First he organized the Nazarene Publishing House in Indianapolis. Later the Nazarene Publishing House in Kansas City purchased his company and his series of songs. More than three thousand Christian songs have the Lillenas name on them. These include "Wonderful Grace of Jesus," "It Is Glory Just to Walk with Him," "I Know a Name," and "In the Garden of My Heart."

Little biographical information is known of Bertha Mae Lillenas. Under the Rodeheaver copyright, she wrote "Jesus Is Always There." Her song "Jesus Took My Burden and Left Me with a Song" became a favorite throughout the United States.[11]

Ira B. Wilson

Phil Kerr, a composer of gospel songs, visited Ira B. Wilson in his California home. Wilson invited Kerr to sit at the piano and sing something. Soon the visitor modulated into what should have been a familiar song to its author. Wilson listened attentively, but the song seemed unfamiliar to him. When Kerr reminded Wilson that he had written it, he appeared startled. Indeed, the lyrics of the frequently used young people's song, "Make Me a Blessing," came from his own pen. The fact that he usually wrote the music rather than the lyrics might help account for his lack of remembering.

From 1905 until his death on April 3, 1950, Ira Wilson spent most of his time writing anthems, cantatas, and oratorios for the Lorenz Publishing Company. Wilson was born in Iowa near "the little brown church in the wildwood."

George S. Schuler

George S. Schuler served on the faculty of his alma mater, Moody Bible Institute, for thirty years. He taught organ, piano, conducting, and harmony. His own musical education included such instructors as Charles H. Gabriel, E. O. Excell, and D. B. Towner. He produced a number of textbooks, including *Evangelistic Hymn Playing*, *Choral Conducting*, and *The Accompanist's Manual*. He also contributed five collections of his song compositions. Schuler made frequent appearances in Winona Lake at the Rodeheaver School of Sacred Music. In his classroom instruction he had the knack of imitating the students at the keyboard, motivating them to feel more relaxed in their performance. During his later years he made his home in Florida. His gospel song "Oh, What a Day!" has the Rodeheaver Company label.[12]

Charles F. Weigle

Composed in 1932 and copyrighted by the Rodeheaver Hall-Mack Company, "No One Ever Cared for Me Like Jesus" by Charles F. Weigle has been a favorite of many gospel singers and radio artists. It has been most effective in evangelistic campaigns, jails, and street meetings. One could feel the emotional response as Mr. Weigle would sing it. He had a special way of rendering the feeling that touched the heart.

A young man sentenced to be electrocuted heard this song sung in a Pennsylvania jail. As a result, he accepted Christ as his Savior. He sang the song day and night up to the time of his execution. At the scheduled hour of his death, this young man was led away to the chamber singing loudly, "No one ever cared for me like Jesus; there's no other friend so kind as He." This testimony must have had a profound effect on inmates and wardens alike.

Weigle was born in Lafayette, Indiana. After his musical training at the Cincinnati Conservatory of Music, he became an evangelistic singer. Later he felt the call to preach. For a number of years he traveled throughout the United States singing, composing music, and preaching.[13]

George Webster

One afternoon in 1923 George Webster was meditating about the religious controversy between modernists and Fundamentalists. He thought, "How much they all need Jesus!" Then came the thought, "How much I need Jesus!" Shortly afterward, he wrote the hymn poem, "I Need Jesus."

Webster was born in New York on April 26, 1866, the son of a Baptist preacher. His conversion took place when he was twenty-one. He spent five years as editor of a local newspaper and then was ordained to the Baptist ministry. He served pastorates in Indiana and Vermont. During the last eighteen years of his life, he served a federated church: the Methodist, Presbyterian, and Baptist church of Essex, New York. He died on October 1, 1942, in Essex.

Webster's first published poem is the familiar "Throw Out the Lifeline." Later Webster worked jointly with hymn composers Isaac Meredith, Peter Billhorn, Charles Gabriel, and Grant Tullar.[14]

Paul Rader

On one occasion Paul Rader was walking across one of Chicago's busiest streets. His four-year-old daughter was walking with him holding tightly to his hand, seemingly unaware of oncoming traffic.

"Aren't you afraid to cross the street?" he asked.

"No," she replied, "Not when you're with me. Why should I be afraid?"

Later it occurred to Rader that Christians should have the same childlike faith in the Lord Jesus Christ. After he returned home, he found his pianist, Lance Latham, and dictated the words and music of the familiar gospel song, "Only Believe."

Paul Rader was born in 1879. In his younger days he was a scholar, an athlete, and a businessman. After his conversion, he was called to the ministry and became one of his generation's outstanding preachers and lecturers. He became the international president of the Christian and Missionary Alliance, and he pastored the Moody Church in Chicago. Later he founded the Chicago Gospel Tabernacle and a missions organization. He was a pioneer in radio broadcasting, and he gave music an important place in his ministry. He died in Hollywood, California, in July of 1938.[15]

W. C. Poole

During the session of a Methodist conference in Wilmington, Delaware, Reverend Taylor, a retired minister, rose to testify. He spoke of his love for his Lord and his thankfulness for having been permitted to have a long, enjoyable ministry. He emphatically stated that he was not approaching an end or a sunset of life. He was waiting expectantly for a "homeward call." He was expecting a sunrise, a beginning of eternal rewards. One minister who heard that testimony, William C. Poole, was inspired to write the lyrics of "Sunrise Tomorrow." Poole died in January of 1950.[16]

Avis B. Christiansen and Harry Dixon Loes

Harry Dixon Loes said that many of his thoughts for gospel songs came from the preaching of Paul Rader. On one occasion Rader preached on John 3:16, stressing man's depravity and the fact that God found a way to bring man back to Himself and that love found a way through God's only son, Jesus Christ, who died on Calvary to restore man to the family of God.

Immediately the phrase "love found a way" impressed Loes as a fine idea for a song. He jotted the pitches on a piece of paper, as well as a few lyric ideas for the chorus. Later he sent the lyric suggestions to Mrs. Avis Burgeson Christiansen in Chicago. She wrote both the stanzas and the chorus.

Harry Dixon Loes, from Michigan, graduated from Moody Bible Institute in 1915 and entered the field of evangelism. In 1939 he became a faculty member at Moody Bible Institute. His well-known gospel songs also include "All Things in Jesus I Find."

Avis Christiansen was born in Chicago. She began writing in 1915 when she heard Loes' song "All Things in Jesus I Find." She produced hundreds of hymn poems, including "It Is Glory Just to Walk with Him" and "Precious Hiding Place."[17]

George Duffield

The winter of 1857-58 will always be known for the wonderful spiritual revival that spread over the land and that was especially strong in the

Philadelphia area. Dudley A. Tyng was a young man with a winsome personality who desired to win souls and was always standing up for Jesus. On one occasion he preached to five thousand on the text "Go now, ye that are men, and serve the Lord" (Exod. 10:11), and a thousand men received Jesus Christ as Savior.

Two weeks later, Tyng returned to his home in the country. He left his desk to look for a corn shelling machine pulled by mules. His sleeve caught in the cogs of the machine, and his arm was badly lacerated. His wounds turned out to be fatal. At daybreak he said to his father and his relatives, "Sing, sing!" Young Dudley began singing "Rock of Ages," and then with the last of his strength he said, "Tell them to stand up for Jesus."

After returning from the memorial service for his close friend, Reverend George Duffield wrote the words of "Stand Up, Stand Up for Jesus." Duffield was born in Pennsylvania in September, 1818, and he died in New Jersey on July 6, 1888. In addition to Duffield himself, his grandfather, his father, and his son were all ministers.[18]

Mrs. C. H. Morris

Mrs. C. H. Morris was among the many hymn writers who were physically handicapped. Mrs. Morris wrote such beloved compositions as "Sweeter As the Years Go By," "The Fight Is On," "Nearer, Still Nearer," and "Let Jesus Come into Your Heart."

Mrs. Morris was born in Ohio in 1862. She was converted at the age of ten, and she became a Methodist. As a child she developed interest and ability as a poet. She was reportedly an unassuming housewife and deeply religious. She kept a writing pad tacked up in her kitchen, and she often did her hymn writing while she was going about her housework. She became totally blind after reaching adulthood, and most of her best gospel songs were written after her affliction.[19]

Will L. Thompson

Will Thompson was born in East Liverpool, Ohio, on November 7, 1847; and he died there on September 20, 1909. While he was a student at the Boston Conservatory of Music, he wrote a number of secular songs. One of them, "Gathering Up the Shells by the Seashore," earned him a small fortune. "The Old Tramp" and "Drifting with the Tide" made him famous. Later he began to publish sacred music: *Thompson's Popular Anthems*, *The Young People's Choir*, and *Enduring Hymns*. "Softly and Tenderly" is still a well-loved song.

Shortly before Dwight L. Moody's death, Thompson became seriously ill. Reaching out a trembling hand, D. L. Moody said, "Will, I would rather have written 'Softly and Tenderly' than [do] anything I have been able to do in my whole life."[20]

James Rowe

B. D. Ackley was vacationing in Winona Lake, Indiana, during June of 1911. One day Charles Gabriel visited him. Ackley played two song tunes that he had recently composed, and he asked for Gabriel's opinion. Gabriel suggested that the chorus of the first tune would go well with the verse of the second tune. Ackley accepted this suggestion, and later this combination became the musical setting for James Rowe's poem "I Walk with the King."

James Rowe was born in England in 1866. Beginning at age 20, he was employed by the Irish government for four years, and then he moved to America. He was employed by a New York railroad for ten years, and finally he became superintendent of a humane society. It has been said that he wrote nine thousand poems, hymns, recitations, and magazine articles, and that many of them were published. Besides "I Walk with the King," a well-known gospel song is "Love Lifted Me."[21]

Frank E. Graeff

Frank E. Graeff was the pastor of a Methodist church in the Philadelphia conference. He was called a "sunshine minister" because of his spiritual optimism. His sunny personality attracted children and adults. However, in spite of his cheery disposition, he was called upon to go through some severe trials. He felt inspired to write the song poem "Does Jesus Care?" He wrote many poems, more than two hundred hymns, and the book called *The Minister's Twins*.

The musical setting to "Does Jesus Care?" was written by J. Lincoln Hall. Hall was born on November 4, 1866, in Philadelphia. He graduated from the University of Philadelphia and later received the Doctor of Music degree. He was known for writing many cantatas and gospel songs, besides editing many hymnals. He possessed unusual ability as both song leader and choral conductor.[22]

Thoro Harris

Numerous gospel songs came from the pen of Thoro Harris, including "He's Coming Soon" and "Give Me Oil in My Lamp." He was a successful hymnbook publisher, whose total circulation was extensive. "He's Coming Soon" was originally sponsored by Haldor Lillenas, but later it was assigned to the Rodeheaver Company.

Harris was born in Washington, D.C., in 1874. His earliest memory is having composed a melody at four years of age (a melody that was published some years later). By the time he was ten, he had written many tunes in a blank music book that he kept for that purpose. At the age of eleven he developed a shorthand system of musical notation, so that he was able to jot down music as quickly as it was sung.

In 1902 Harris went to Boston, where he completed his first hymnal. Later he moved to Chicago and spent some successful time there, meeting many musical personalities such as Peter Bilhorn, James Rowe, and Lizzie DeArmond. He spent his later years in Eureka Springs, Arkansas. He died on March 25, 1955.[23]

W. Roland Felts

Roland Felts lived a most unusual life musically. At the age of 15, he was a church organist and pianist. Later he became the music director of a local radio station in Nashville, Tennessee. He was part of a quartet that sang in various churches. He served as a musician for fifty years.

During the summer of 1951, Roland Felts met Homer Rodeheaver during a week of camp meetings at a Methodist conference grounds at Lake Junaluska. Having just been discharged from the armed services, Felts accompanied a music director named Cyrus Daniels to Junaluska. Before entering the armed services, Roland had sung in quartets from Daniels's choir. When Rodeheaver met Felts, the young man did not yet have a job for the coming fall.

Rodeheaver suggested that Felts come to Winona Lake, travel with him, and be with him during the summer months. After finishing college at Asbury, Felts returned to the Rodeheaver Company to work as an associate music director. He did this until the death of B. D. Ackley in 1958. After that, Felts served as music editor until the sale of the Rodeheaver Hall-Mack Company in 1969 to Word Incorporated.

Roland Felts expressed these comments about Rodeheaver: "It was a pleasure to live as closely as I did with Rody during those last years. I found him to be a considerate, charming, personable Christian, a gentleman of the highest order. Having known and worked with a person like Rody has been a lasting influence on my life."[24]

Notes

Chapter 1

1. Tullis, Dan. "Front Row, Center," *Everyday Religion*. 1950.

2. Rodeheaver, Homer. "Humble Beginnings at an Early Age." Leaflet, M. M. Cole, 1933.

3. Rodeheaver, Homer. *Singing Black*. Chicago: Rodeheaver Company, 1936.

4. Ibid.

5. Tullis, Dan. "Front Row, Center," *Everyday Religion*. 1950.

Chapter 2

1. Rodeheaver, H. with R. A. Walton and W. Biederwolf. "Rodeheaver's Ministry." Unpublished manuscript, 1933.

2. Rodeheaver, Homer. *Singing Black*. Chicago: Rodeheaver Company, 1936.

3. Ibid.

4. Rodeheaver, Homer. Unpublished diary, 1923-24.

5. Ibid.

6. Rodeheaver, Homer. *Twenty Years with Billy Sunday*. Winona Lake, IN: Rodeheaver Hall-Mack Company, 1936.

7. Rodeheaver, Homer. Unpublished diary, 1923-24.

Chapter 3

1. Heaton, James. *History of Winona Lake*. The Westminster Hotel. Brochure.
2. Ibid.
3. Heaton, James. *History of Winona Lake*. The Westminster Hotel. Brochure.
4. Ibid.

Chapter 4

1. Rodeheaver, Homer. *Twenty Years with Billy Sunday*. Winona Lake, IN: Rodeheaver Hall-Mack Company, 1936.
2. Ibid.
3. Ibid.
4. Ibid.
5. *More Worthwhile Poems*. ed. Homer Rodeheaver. Winona Lake, IN: Rodeheaver Hall-Mack Company, 1945.
6. Rodeheaver, Homer. *F'r Instance: 450 Choice Selections of Anecdotes and Illustrations for Public Speakers*. Winona Lake, IN: Rodeheaver Hall-Mack Company, 1947.
7. Dorsett, Lyle W. *Billy Sunday and the Redemption of Urban America*. Grand Rapids: William B. Eerdmans Publishing Company, 1991.

8. Ibid.

9. Ibid.

10. Rodeheaver, Homer. *Twenty Years with Billy Sunday*. Winona Lake, IN: Rodeheaver Hall-Mack Company, 1936.

11. Butterfield, Roger. "Homer Rodeheaver: A Happy Christian with an Old Trombone Is Successfully Preaching Salvation Through Song." *Life*, (1945), p. 65.

12. Ibid.

13. Gladdis, V. H., and J. A. Huffman. *The Story of Winona Lake: A Memory and a Vision*. Butler, IN: Higley Huffman Press, 1960.

14. Dorsett, Lyle W. *Billy Sunday and the Redemption of Urban America*. Grand Rapids: William B. Eerdmans Publishing Company, 1991.

15. Ibid.

16. Ibid.

17. Ibid.

18. Ibid.

19. Rodeheaver, Homer. *Twenty Years with Billy Sunday*. Winona Lake, IN: Rodeheaver Hall-Mack Company, 1936.

Chapter 6

1. Rodeheaver, Homer. "Training of Two Korean Brothers." Unpublished manuscript.

2. Roosevelt, Franklin D. Quote from a personalized calandar. 1990.

3. Decca Album 64. "Decca Presents Homer A. Rodeheaver." Brochure.

4. Sanville, George. "Rody's Mass Leadership." Brochure.

5. Sanville, George. "Homer Rodeheaver [and] Ruth Rodeheaver Thomas." Concert publicity flier.

6. Jones, Bob. *Cornbread and Caviar.* Greenville, SC: Bob Jones University Press, 1985.

7. Rodeheaver, Homer. "A Nation-Wide Challenge: The Liquor Traffic." Unpublished manuscript, 1947.

8. Dorsett, Lyle W. *Billy Sunday and the Redemption of Urban America.* Grand Rapids: William B. Eerdmans Publishing Company, 1991.

9. Butterfield, Roger. "Homer Rodeheaver: A Happy Christian with an Old Trombone Is Successfully Preaching Salvation Through Song." *Life*, (1945), p. 65.

Chapter 7

1. Rodeheaver, Homer. "Contact with a Potential Music Student." Unpublished manuscript.

2. Rodeheaver, Homer. "General Conference of Pastors and Musicians." Unpublished manuscript.

3. Gruss, Edmond C. *Cults and the Occult*, 3rd ed. Phillipsburg, NJ: Presbyterian and Reformed Publishing Company, 1974.

Chapter 8

1. Rodeheaver, Homer. *Song Leadership*. Winona Lake, IN: Rodeheaver Hall-Mack Company, 1941.

2. Ibid.

3. Ibid.

Chapter 9

1. "A Little Prayer," *Worthwhile Poems*. Chicago: Rodeheaver Company, 1916.

Chapter 10

1. Kerr, Phil. *Music in Evangelism*. Grand Rapids: Zondervan Publishing Company, 1962.

2. Ibid.

3. Ibid.

4. Ibid.

5. Ibid.

6. Ibid.

7. Ibid.

8. Ibid.

9. Tarr, Leslie K. "Oswald J. Smith: Obsessed and Possessed with Getting Every Soul to

Christ." *Fundamentalist Journal*, (1987), pp. 44-45.

10. Hoke, Donald E. *Life Story of Harry Ironside*. Grand Rapids: Zondervan Publishing Company.

11. Kerr, Phil. *Music in Evangelism*. Grand Rapids: Zondervan Publishing Company, 1962.

12. Ibid.

13. Ibid.

14. Ibid.

15. Ibid.

16. Ibid.

17. Ibid.

18. Ibid.

19. Ibid.

20. Ibid.

21. Ibid.

22. Ibid.

23. Ibid.

24. Felts, Roland. Unpublished letter, 1997.